BARN

First broadcast on the 20th November 1959, on the B.B.C. Third Programme, and subsequently produced at the Questors Theatre, Ealing, on the 13th June 1960.

CHARACTERS

(in the order of their appearance)

HELEN CARBOY

CHARLES CARBOY, her father

THE REVEREND WANDSWORTH TEETER

DAPHNE CARBOY, Charles's wife

SANDRA, the maid

The action of the Play passes in the drawing-room of the Carboys' home on a spring morning

BARNSTABLE

First broadcast on the 20th November 1950 on the B.B.C. Third Programme, and subsequently produced at the Queen's Theatre, Ealing, on the 13th June 1900.

CHARACTERS

(in the order of their appearance)

HELEN CARBOY

CHARLES CARBOY, her father

THE REVEREND WADSWORTH TARTER

DAPHNE CARBOY, Charles's wife

SANDRA, the maid

The action of the Play passes in the drawing-room of the Carboys' home on a spring morning.

BARNSTABLE

SCENE—*The drawing-room of the Carboys' home on a spring morning.*

The door is R, *the fireplace is back* C, *and there are french windows* L, *opening on to a lawn. There is a sofa* RC, *a round table* C *and an armchair* LC. *Another table stands down* L. *Over the fireplace is a large gilt-framed portrait of a Caroline drinking party. Other suitable dressing can be added at the discretion of the producer.*

When the CURTAIN *rises, the room is lit by the morning sun which streams through the french windows.* HELEN *is standing at the french windows, looking out, wrapped in thought. Two thrushes are heard singing.* HELEN *looks up at the sky. There is the sound of a shot. The song of one thrush stops abruptly. There is another shot and the second thrush falls silent.*

HELEN. Oh, God!

(There is a moment's pause.
CHARLES CARBOY, Helen's father, enters R.
THE REVEREND WANDSWORTH TEETER follows him on. CARBOY *is in plus-fours, and unremarkable, neither portly nor slim, looking as though chronic indigestion suits him well. He carries a dead mole by the tail.* TEETER *is collared)*

CARBOY *(crossing to* R *of the table* C*)* It's not right, you know, and it worries me. Nothing you could put your finger on, you understand, I couldn't give a diagnosis; in fact to be quite honest, I'm not even sure about the symptoms. But I'm convinced it's not as it should be.

TEETER *(moving down* RC*)* Well, well!

CARBOY. That's all very fine, but you're not personally involved. You're just a bystander.

(HELEN closes the french windows, turns impulsively, goes to the telephone on the table C, *lifts the receiver and dials a number.*

CARBOY *drops the mole on to a copy of the "Spectator" on the same table at the other side of which* HELEN *is at the telephone, though they ignore each other*)

TEETER. Charles, my heart bleeds . . .

CARBOY. Now, now, Wandsworth, I don't blame you. Why *should* you let it trouble you? I know the feeling; I feel precisely the same when I'm in somebody else's garden. I say to myself: "There's some *Stratiotes Sylvaticus* growing over there," and that's an end to it. Not a thought to the health of the thing, not a thought to its owner, who nurtures it. (*He moves to* L *of Teeter*) So I appreciate your point of view, you see.

HELEN (*into the telephone*) I wish to emigrate . . .

CARBOY. But at the same time you must realize that while to you this is just somebody else's *Stratiotes Sylvaticus*, to me it's *my Stratiotes Sylvaticus*, growing in *my* garden. You try saying, "Well, well!" in a case like that. The boot's on the other foot.

HELEN (*into the telephone*) I *am* holding on.

TEETER. I'm sure it'll all turn out for the best.

CARBOY. Ah, but will it?

TEETER. My dear Charles . . .

CARBOY. You're an idealist, Wandsworth, if I may say so, but I'm a realist. I face facts. I look the situation in the eye. And the way I see it is this: the soil's right, the acidity's right, I've had it checked, there's no doubt about the acidity. It's had a nice mild winter.

(HELEN *jiggles the receiver rest*)

I've cloched it, I've watered it, I've sprayed it. It's against the south wall, nicely protected. And yet it's not well. There's something the matter with it. It's not well.

HELEN (*into the telephone*) Hallo. Will you please speak! . . .

CARBOY. And we don't know why. Well, then, perhaps it'll get better, as you say, but I don't see why it should. Why should it? I tell you, quite honestly, I'm worried about that *Stratiotes Sylvaticus*.

HELEN (*into the telephone*) Yes, emigrate, emigrate . . .

TEETER. I wish I could advise you. A message of hope is all I can offer.

HELEN (*into the telephone*) How far can one go? . . .

CARBOY. I shouldn't burden you with my problems.

TEETER. No, no. What are old friends for?

HELEN (*into the telephone*) New Zealand? Is that the farthest? . . .

TEETER. Could it perhaps be the air?

CARBOY. In what way?

TEETER. It's just a thought. You say the soil's all right and the treatment's right and the aspect's right. All that's left really is the air.

HELEN (*into the telephone*) Yes, yes, farther than that . . .

CARBOY (*after a moment's thought*) The *air*—now that's a new line of approach, certainly.

HELEN (*into the telephone*) Fiji is useless. Farther! Farther! . . .

TEETER. Something in the air perhaps . . .

HELEN (*into the telephone*) Is there nowhere unknown, is there nowhere? . . .

CARBOY. Which . . .

TEETER. Tends to, perhaps . . .

HELEN (*into the telephone*) It doesn't matter. (*She replaces the receiver*)

CARBOY. But it was all right last year. I tell you, the soil's right, the acidity's right . . .

HELEN (*with a sob*) Oh, God!

(CARBOY *and* TEETER *turn and look at Helen*)

TEETER. My dear Miss Carboy . . .

HELEN. I'm terribly sorry, it's most idiotic of me. I don't know what has come over me. It's really most frightfully idiotic of me, I'm really most frightfully sorry. (*She crosses to the door* R) I must write a letter.

(HELEN *exits* R)

CARBOY. It had a nice mild winter. It's sheltered from the wind . . .

TEETER. Is something troubling Helen?

CARBOY. Who?

TEETER. Your daughter is not herself.

CARBOY. I believe she's worried about young Bob.

TEETER. Young Bob, eh?

CARBOY. You know young Bob?

TEETER. I know *a* young Bob. Whether the same one . . .

CARBOY. The same, the same. Her brother.

TEETER. Tck, tck, tck!

CARBOY. Well, well! (*He pauses*) And now moles under the lawn. (*He indicates the dead mole*) What can one do?

TEETER. Young Bob, eh?

CARBOY. I'll get some of the air in the garden analysed, of course, but I don't see what good it'll do.

TEETER. Well, well—the Lord giveth and the Lord taketh away.

CARBOY. What *does* one do about moles?

TEETER. Block up their burrows?

CARBOY. Where there's one mole there'll be another.

TEETER. Or arsenic.

CARBOY. And how does one get the air into the bottle?

(DAPHNE CARBOY *appears outside the french windows. She carries an armful of flowers. She tries to open the window. Finding rattling useless, she kicks at the door. Her first two kicks hit the door, but the third puts her foot through one of the lower panes of glass*)

TEETER. I believe Daphne wants to come in.

CARBOY. Who?

TEETER. Your wife.

CARBOY. I'm worried about this mole, you know. (*He crosses to the french windows and tries to open them*)

TEETER (*crossing to* L *of the table* C *and looking at the dead mole*) This one?

CARBOY (*struggling with the windows*) I mean its implications. Greenfly is one thing; but when things—start coming up at you—from under the ground—it's something else again. (*He stops trying to open the windows for a moment*) At least worms are discreet about it.

TEETER. They are all God's creatures.

CARBOY (*struggling with the windows*) Well, now, I don't

want to lay the blame anywhere. I just want them out—
from under my—lawn. (*He manages to wrench the windows
open*)

(DAPHNE *enters by the french windows and crosses to* C)

DAPHNE. Charles, I'm worried about Helen.

CARBOY. Yes, dear.

DAPHNE. Wandsworth, how nice to see you so early.
Have you met my husband?

CARBOY (*moving down* L) Twenty years ago!

DAPHNE. Really! As long ago as that?

CARBOY (*embarrassed*) It's always the same, these sunny
mornings.

DAPHNE. How old was I then?

CARBOY. It's immaterial.

DAPHNE. Oh, my poor dear dead husband.

TEETER. Yes, well, yes, well . . . (*He coughs, moves to the
french windows and looks out*)

(CARBOY *moves to* L *of the table* C, *picks up the dead mole
and swings it nervously by the tail*)

DAPHNE. Things were different, then. (*She looks from one
to the other for confirmation*)

(CARBOY *and* TEETER *avoid her eyes*)

Roseate, it was. Halcyon. When my poor dear husband
used to take me by the hand down into the rose garden,
and there we'd sit, with the scent of the roses heavy in the
air and our faces rosy with the setting sun. There we'd sit
without a word till the roses lost their colour and the last
light went from the sky. (*She sobs discreetly*)

CARBOY. It was me.

DAPHNE. Who's that?

CARBOY. I was your husband. You've only had one
husband. Every spring we have this.

DAPHNE (*crossing down* L) There was another, I'm sure
of it.

CARBOY. We have enough on our plate as it is. (*He holds
up the dead mole*) Look at this.

DAPHNE. A vole?

CARBOY. Not a vole—a *mole*.

DAPHNE. Dead?

CARBOY. Would I be holding it by the tail if it were not?

DAPHNE. One holds rabbits by the ears, what do you expect of me? So now he's taken to shooting moles.

CARBOY. Who?

DAPHNE. Barnstable. Who else would shoot moles?

CARBOY. Nonsense, dear! I killed this mole.

DAPHNE. *You* shot it?

CARBOY. Not shot. I hit it with a spade.

DAPHNE. I heard a shot.

CARBOY. How could there be a shot when I hit it with a spade?

DAPHNE. There was a shot.

CARBOY. I heard no shot. You imagined a shot. It was a bird.

DAPHNE. A bird shot?

CARBOY. Not shot! The shot was a bird. Or the wind. Something.

DAPHNE. Shooting of defenceless moles . . .

CARBOY. Not moles! Not moles!

DAPHNE. It comes to the same thing. Two shots rang out, say what you like. If it wasn't a mole it was something else.

(*There is a pause.* DAPHNE *drops her flowers on the table down* L, *takes a pair of secateurs from her pocket and begins to cut the stems*)

CARBOY. You cut flowers. You think nothing of that. You cut them down in their prime. A flower is a flower. Very well, then. If you shot them it would come to the same . . .

(DAPHNE *ignores* CARBOY *who loses interest in the argument and stands idly swinging the dead mole*)

TEETER (*turning from the french windows*) In the midst of one's adversities one should remember one is not alone. Others, too, have had their tribulations. (*He crosses down* R) There was a garden in Hackney Wick where the *Stratiotes Sylvaticus* was never up to standard. He was a God-fearing man, but from one year to the next his *Stratiotes Sylvaticus* was a disappointment.

CARBOY. The soil was wrong, but in *my* case . . .

TEETER. Ah, now, but that is the surprising thing about it; one day the police came and dug up his *Stratiotes Sylvaticus*——

CARBOY. The police?

TEETER. —and discovered that his *wife*—was underneath them all the time.

CARBOY. Well, there you are.

TEETER. Perhaps. But this is the enigma: whether it was his wife's complaining about the state of them which caused him to put her underneath them, or whether his putting her underneath them caused them to lose the will to live.

CARBOY. A sprinkling of bonemeal is all they need. A sprinkling. Mine have had that. But they're not right.

TEETER. God's will be done.

CARBOY. That's all very well.

DAPHNE. I am worried about which vase to put these flowers in. Many small vases, or one large.

(*The telephone rings.* CARBOY *puts down the mole and lifts the receiver*)

CARBOY (*into the telephone*) Yes? . . . No, no, no . . . Now, listen carefully: take *three* of the small red pills twice a day followed by *four* of the large blue pills three times a day . . . In water, in water; and the liniment at blood-heat. Is that clear? . . . Being colour-blind is irrelevant. The red pills are small, the large pills are blue . . . The white pills are for emergencies . . . I'll call on Tuesday, if you're still with us. (*He replaces the receiver*)

TEETER. One wonders that a mole bothers to have a tail at all, it can only be an inconvenience.

CARBOY. She has rubbed the pills on her chest and drunk the liniment. And she's getting better. What do they expect of one?

TEETER (*sitting on the sofa*) You should take a day off occasionally.

CARBOY (*moving* RC) I do. It makes no difference. The mortality rate is the same.

TEETER. Yes, I see that. But if you were to take a day off occasionally . . .

DAPHNE. Charles . . .

CARBOY (*turning to Daphne*) One large vase. (*He turns away*) In water, three times a day.

DAPHNE. Charles, I'm worried about Helen.

CARBOY. Yes, yes.

DAPHNE. Not only that, but I'm also worried about Barnstable.

(CARBOY *looks at Daphne.* TEETER *coughs*)

In fact, I'm worried about Barnstable more than I'm worried about Helen.

(SANDRA, *the maid, enters* R)

CARBOY. What is it, Sandra?

SANDRA (*soundlessly*) If you please, I'm giving notice.

CARBOY. Speak up, speak up.

SANDRA. If you please, I'm giving notice.

CARBOY. Nonsense! You may go. (*He moves to the table* C *and picks up the mole*)

SANDRA (*soundlessly*) I'm sorry.

CARBOY. What?

SANDRA. I'm sorry.

CARBOY. Nonsense! (*He holds up the mole by the tail and speaks to it*) She comes in here without by-your-leave and says she's giving *notice*. (*He turns to Sandra*) You seem to forget what you are. I've a good mind to give you notice.

SANDRA. Oh, sir.

CARBOY. What do you make of it, Wandsworth?

TEETER. Let us not be precipitate. (*To Sandra*) Come here, my child.

(SANDRA *moves to Teeter*)

You may speak freely to me. Are you not happy here?

SANDRA. It's the thrushes, sir.

TEETER. You don't like thrushes?

SANDRA. Last week it was squirrels. Now it's thrushes.

TEETER. What is, my child?

SANDRA. Shot, sir.

CARBOY. Nonsense!

TEETER (*to Carboy*) Hush! (*To Sandra*) Not here, Sandra. Not in this country. You have imagined it all.

SANDRA. They're out there on the lawn.

TEETER. No, no. Imagined, imagined. Fulfil your tasks diligently, Sandra. Girdle your horizons with honest toil. There, you feel better already, don't you?

SANDRA. I don't know, sir.

TEETER. Come to me when you are in trouble. I am an open door.

SANDRA. Yes, sir.

CARBOY. You may go.

SANDRA. What shall I do about the thrushes on the lawn, sir?

CARBOY. Let them lie.

SANDRA. Yes, sir. (*She moves to the door* R)

TEETER (*rising*) Sandra.

SANDRA (*stopping and turning*) Yes, sir?

TEETER. Do you ever speak to strangers?

SANDRA. Not unless I know them, sir.

TEETER. If you should, and they should tell you things . . .

SANDRA. Oh, sir!

TEETER. Believe them not.

SANDRA. Yes, sir.

TEETER. All is as it seems. Let that be your golden thought. Carry it with you like a banner. All is as it seems.

SANDRA. Yes, sir.

TEETER. Birds, too, have their resting-place, their haven.

SANDRA. Yes, sir.

TEETER. You may go.

SANDRA. Yes, sir.

CARBOY. And let it not occur again.

SANDRA. No, sir. (*She turns to go*)

DAPHNE. Sandra.

SANDRA (*turning*) Yes, madam?

DAPHNE. Bring me a vase. One large vase.

SANDRA. Yes, ma'am.

(SANDRA *exits* R)

TEETER. Tck, tck, tck, tck, tck, tck!

CARBOY. No taste; no tact.

TEETER. Nearer the earth, of course.

CARBOY. It's ingrained in them.

TEETER. She does her best, perhaps.

CARBOY. That's not the point.

TEETER. Well no.

(*There is a pause*)

DAPHNE. So it's thrushes, now.

CARBOY. What?

DAPHNE. Sandra is right. Last week it was squirrels. This week it's thrushes. Where's it all going to end?

CARBOY. Thrushes, squirrels, it makes no difference.

DAPHNE. It seems hard . . .

CARBOY. The thrushes must look after themselves. The world is what it is.

TEETER. One should, moreover, bear this in mind: man is but a grain of sand in the desert. The desert has its reason and its purpose, but what does the grain of sand know of that, parched and trodden underfoot by the pads of itinerant camels? There is a benevolence all unbeknownst. The thrush falls; why? Who can tell? Reason, purpose, nevertheless, must there be. The chafing babe cries, but maternal wisdom presides. We chafe, we fret, we question; only the mind-blind bird, unquestioning, blissful sings.

(*A shot is heard. The mind-blind bird gives up singing*)

DAPHNE. Another.

TEETER. And I must go.

CARBOY. So soon?

TEETER (*crossing to the french windows*) I must keep moving. To spread comfort.

DAPHNE. You are a good man.

TEETER. Life must go on.

(TEETER *exits by the french windows.* CARBOY *puts the dead mole on the table* C *and crosses to* RC)

DAPHNE. He is such a comfort.

CARBOY. I'm worried about the *Stratiotes Sylvaticus*. And the moles.

DAPHNE. I'm worried about Helen and young Bob.

CARBOY. I'm worried about old Mrs Fagoty. If she loses her head and takes the white pills, she's done for. And I'm worried about the moles.

DAPHNE. I'm worried about Charles, he worries too much.

CARBOY. I'm worried about the lease of the house.

DAPHNE. I'm worried about that vase.

CARBOY. Only another forty-three years, and then what? It just goes to show, one should never take out a ninety-nine-year lease. A *nine hundred* and ninety-nine-year lease, now, there's *stability*. Well, well, we shall know next time.

DAPHNE. I'm worried about Sandra.

CARBOY. I'm worried about whether to clean my teeth before shaving and then wash, or wash before cleaning my teeth and then shave, and I'm worried about whether to wear my shirt-tail outside my underpants for comfort or inside my underpants for security.

DAPHNE. I'm worried about Helen.

CARBOY. I'm worried about old Mrs Fagoty. Should I ring her up? After all, she's seventy-eight.

DAPHNE. And the vase.

CARBOY. I'm worried about whether to ring her up.

DAPHNE. And Helen and Sandra.

CARBOY. If only she weren't on the phone. Why did I ever give her the white pills in the first place? I must have been mad. It isn't as though she needs the pills. Red, white and blue pills, she could do without the lot. And the liniment. There's nothing wrong with her that old age won't cure. As long as she doesn't take the pills. If she died tomorrow nobody would mind, least of all old Mrs Fagoty. Unless she dies of the white pills. Then some busy-body will come and look inside her stomach. Find it chock-ful of white pills. Ask me why I *gave* her the white pills. I don't know why I gave her the white pills. I don't even remember what she was suffering from, apart from living. Insomnia, pains in the—shoulder, I haven't the faintest idea. What was *in* the white pills? I don't know. Maybe she'll leave them in the kitchen and the cat will get them. One can but hope. What they'll do to her cat is not my business. I'm no vet. Turn it into a dog, perhaps. Or is it a dog she has already? It's called Agamemnon, that I remember. Would that be a cat or a dog? Dear God, let old Mrs Fagoty die of old age.

DAPHNE. And Barnstable. And Barnstable. And Barnstable . . .

CARBOY (*exasperated*) My dear Daphne, here we are with moles under our very lawn and you . . .

(*There is a long, sad, rumbling sound, culminating in a crash. A piece of plaster falls from the ceiling*)

DAPHNE. There!

CARBOY. I don't follow your reasoning.

DAPHNE. Another chimney falling. It's all this shooting.

CARBOY. Not necessarily.

DAPHNE. Do you deny it?

CARBOY. One must look at both sides of the question.

DAPHNE. Ever since the shooting started chimneys have been falling.

CARBOY. Chimneys have always been falling. The week we arrived a chimney fell. They've been falling ever since. It's a law of nature. Depreciation. What can one expect?

DAPHNE. But not so frequently.

CARBOY (*moving* C) When he used to stamp to and fro in his boots you said that was making the chimneys fall; now he shoots thrushes you say that makes the chimneys fall. It needs nothing. Chimneys fall. It's a law of nature. That's all there is to it. They stand up and then after a time they fall down. Depreciation. What do you expect of a chimney? Chimneys are only human, like the rest of us.

DAPHNE. Last week a shot rang out and then a chimney fell.

CARBOY. Not at all. On the contrary. Your memory is at fault, Daphne. A: you say a shot rang out and then a chimney fell. On the contrary, a chimney fell and then a shot rang out. B: it was not a chimney at all. You *said* it was a chimney, just as you thought it fell after the shot rang out whereas in *fact*, on the contrary, it fell before the shot rang out and it was not a chimney at all but the roof of the west wing. If you will cast your mind back . . .

DAPHNE. Are you suggesting that it was the roof of the west wing falling in which caused the shot to ring out?

CARBOY. Not at all. Neither am I saying that it is my *Stratiotes Sylvaticus* which is causing the moles to burrow under the lawn.

DAPHNE. Moles always burrow under lawns. It's a law of nature.

CARBOY. Exactly. The crux of my argument.

DAPHNE. Oh.

CARBOY. And chimneys have to fall.

DAPHNE. But not so frequently.

CARBOY. Yes, yes as frequently. It's a law of nature. In any case, you were wrong once, you may be wrong again. You say it's a chimney. How do you know it's a chimney?

DAPHNE. It sounded like a chimney.

CARBOY. When the roof of the west wing fell in you said it sounded like a chimney. It was a roof, nevertheless. This may be a chimney. But it may be a roof. We don't know, Daphne, we just don't know. Let us be realistic.

DAPHNE. It sounded more like a chimney than a roof to me.

CARBOY. When the roof of the west wing fell in you said . . .

(*There is another long, sad, rumbling sound, culminating in a crash. A piece of plaster falls from the ceiling*)

DAPHNE. There! Another!

CARBOY. There's no arguing with you.

DAPHNE. It's Barnstable, Barnstable!

CARBOY. Not necessarily.

(HELEN *enters* R. DAPHNE *begins to arrange her flowers on the table* L. CARBOY *picks up the dead mole*)

HELEN (*moving* RC) I wish to apologize for making an exhibition of myself.

DAPHNE. What, dear?

HELEN. Father, I wish to apologize for making an . . .

CARBOY. Yes, yes. Life's full enough as it is . . .

HELEN. It was absolutely idiotic of me. I don't know how I can ever forgive myself for being so absolutely idiotic——

CARBOY. It's over and done with.

HELEN. —and fatuous.

(CARBOY *shrugs in embarrassment*)

And inane, absolutely fatuous and inane. I feel absolutely idiotic. I don't know what Wandsworth Teeter must have thought of me.

CARBOY. Nothing, nothing.

HELEN. He must have thought me absolutely fatuous and inane and idiotic. After all, he is so absolutely marvellous and good.

(*There is a silence*)

He's so absolutely mature and sensible and kind. I feel as though I could crawl under his feet, he's so good and so kind and I made an absolutely fatuous exhibition of myself.

(CARBOY *swings the mole frantically.* DAPHNE *looks on in bewilderment*)

(*She crosses to the french windows*) The sun is shining straight down on to the garden.

CARBOY. The grass isn't ready for it, yet.

HELEN. Just as though nothing will happen. (*She pauses*) Harold has asked me to go out riding with Peggy and Oscar this afternoon, to meet Cyril and Betty and then play squash at Robin's; but Robin is playing croquet at David's with Meryl and Cedric, and Cecil can't come because of his cousin Agnes who's a bad sailor; but if I go boating with Mervyn and Gilbert they'll bring Rosemary and Perkin, and he'll bring Humphrey and Leslie and Lavinia and Claire, and Claire will bring Timothy and Elspeth. If only I had a real *friend*: they are all so—idiotic. Fatuous, terribly inane, I feel so idiotically lonely and inane and inane and Wandsworth Teeter is so big and so strong and so kind and so terribly—*understanding*, the sun is shining all over the lawn, is there going to be a storm or something terrible or what, oh God! Mother, I'm worried about Ernest.

DAPHNE. Ernest, dear?

HELEN. He has asked me to marry him.

DAPHNE. What, after you've been engaged to him for five years?

HELEN. Why can't people accept things as they are?

CARBOY. It's the thin edge of the wedge. He gets engaged and the next minute he wants to get married. He'll be setting up house with you next, mark my words.

HELEN. It's so terribly humiliating and—*degrading*.

CARBOY. And share his meals with you. It'll come to that.

HELEN. Why is everything so terribly involved and—and —*sordid?* Once he touched my hand with his finger. I felt utterly humiliated and wretched. I lay on my bed for three days staring at the ceiling and feeling utterly humiliated and—and—*unclean*. There are dead thrushes all over the lawn. And the roof of the east wing has fallen in.

CARBOY. Nonsense!

HELEN. It's true. I saw it fall.

DAPHNE. Well, well, it's put itself right again, I dare say.

CARBOY. Things are never as bad as they seem.

HELEN. If only I could stop thinking. Father, I think there is somebody living upstairs.

CARBOY. What?

DAPHNE. Hush, dear.

HELEN. I've heard his footsteps. *He* shoots the thrushes.

CARBOY. Nonsense, nonsense!

DAPHNE. How could there be, dear?

CARBOY. Exactly. How could there be anyone living upstairs—when there *aren't any stairs?* There are *moles* on the lawn. The lawn is covered with moles. You mistook them for thrushes. It's perfectly obvious. Here is the proof. (*He holds up the mole*)

DAPHNE. Now, why don't you have a nice cup of cocoa and go to bed?

HELEN. How can I go to bed when the roof has fallen on to my bedroom?

DAPHNE. Shall we have a game of Ludo together?

HELEN. No, no. Perhaps I shall drive into town with Malcolm. Only he's incomprehensible. What shall I do? Shall I stay home and write inane letters to people I despise? Shall I pick flowers?

DAPHNE. No more flowers, we're swamped as it is.

HELEN. Sometimes I think I shall go mad, mad. If only I could. Mother, am I going mad, is that it?

CARBOY (*moving* RC) When I was a boy I loved nothing better than to sleep on the roof in fine weather. Now, wait —if I were to bury hypodermic needles all over the lawn, that would give them something to think about.

HELEN. Something is going to happen, something absolutely inane and dreadful is going to happen, what shall I do? There's a sort of impending doom. Shall I fish, shall I pick flowers? Shall I paint water-colours in the garden? What do I know that no-one else knows?

(*There is a crash*)

DAPHNE. Well, *that* was a chimney-pot, come what may.

(SANDRA *enters* R. *She is wheeling a trolley on which is an enormous vase*)

SANDRA (*soundlessly*) If you please, sir . . .

CARBOY. Speak up, my girl.

SANDRA. If you please, sir, the east wing has fallen.

CARBOY. Nonsense, nonsense! Learn your place, my girl.

DAPHNE. Bring it over here, Sandra.

(SANDRA *wheels the trolly to* L)

You may pick flowers, now, Helen. As many as you like. Pick *all* the flowers. We shall arrange a centrepiece for the dining-room.

SANDRA. The dining-room's gone, ma'am.

CARBOY. Gone?

SANDRA. Fallen, sir.

CARBOY. Nonsense, nonsense! It's all these paperbacks, that's the cause of it. Apply yourself, my girl. Be diligent.

Cast your eye downwards. Humility. Sacrifice. How dare you! Remember your place!

(*There is a crash. Plaster falls from the ceiling*)

DAPHNE. More frequently.

SANDRA. Oh, sir.

CARBOY. Nonsense! It was nothing. A bird falling. Let us at all events keep calm.

HELEN. It's coming. Shall I read a book? Shall I attempt a potato-cut? Shall I knit an Alpine pullover? (*She turns to face the room. Hysterically*) I wish to give notice that I hereby disclaim responsibility for all debts incurred by members of my family.

(*There is a tremendous crash. The pictures on the wall up* C, *falls. The* LIGHTS BLACK-OUT. *The dialogue continues in the* BLACK-OUT)

SANDRA. Sir, I wish to give notice.

CARBOY. Keep calm, kindly keep calm.

(*There is a pause*)

(*He strikes a match*) Let us keep our heads. My assessment of the situation is this: the sun appears to have gone temporarily out. That is all. I have no doubt that it will be remedied in due course of time. (*His match goes out*) Meanwhile, we must do the best we can to behave as Englishmen.

DAPHNE. Should we perhaps switch *our* lights on?

CARBOY. No, no. Better not to meddle with the course of nature. One doesn't burn electricity in broad daylight.

(*There is a pause.*

DAPHNE *exits* R *and* HELEN *exits* L *in the* BLACK-OUT. SANDRA *sits in the armchair* LC *and sobs*)

Be quiet, my girl. Learn your place. To be English is everything. When I was in the trenches, in nineteen-fifteen, my imperturbability was a byword. The men had a nickname for me, I remember; they used to call me "Imperturbable Robinson"—why "Robinson" I never discovered. I was, though I say it, an inspiration to the men. "Men," I used to say to them, as we waited for the signal to advance,

"men, in another moment we shall be advancing upon the
enemy through a hail of machine-gun bullets. We shall be
enfiladed from the right, enfiladed from the left, and bom-
barded by mortars from the centre. In the event of our
succeeding in crossing No Man's Land, we shall find our-
selves face to face with enemy bayonets of extreme numeri-
cal superiority. Supposing us to have overcome the enemy
and take up position in their own trenches, we shall doubt-
less find them no less water-logged than our own. The only
apparent difference will be our greater proximity to the
enemy howitzers, which will, of course, bombard our new-
won position. However, let us not lose our sense of proportion."

(*There is a crash of falling masonry*)

"Let us achieve a balanced judgement in the light of an
all-round assessment of the situation——"

(*His last words are drowned by another crash*)

"——bearing in mind our mental limitations."

(*There is another crash, and a scream cut short*)

My subaltern once told me he would rather be blown up
under me than under any other commanding officer. As
indeed he was.

(*The* LIGHTS *come up. The scene is one of desolation. The
french windows at which Helen was standing are missing, as is
the wall, as is Helen. There is a heap of masonry in their place,
past which is a fine view over the garden.* DAPHNE *is nowhere
to be seen.* SANDRA *is sitting in the armchair* LC, *crying quietly.*
CARBOY *is standing* RC)

His name was "Partridge" and he lived at Palmer's Green.
His widow was a charming lady.

(TEETERS *enters* L, *picking his way through what were once
the french windows*)

And of great fortitude. "Well, well," she said, "as long as

he was not blown up in vain, all is for the best." "Blown up in vain!" I said. "Dear lady, we captured a hundred yards of trench."

TEETER (*moving* C *and declaiming*) My soul was stricken with great guilt!

CARBOY. It is at times like these that the mettle shows. To be British is everything.

TEETER. Where is Helen?

CARBOY (*looking around*) Gone to ground, gone to ground.

TEETER. There was a cry. Who needs me?

(SANDRA *sobs*)

(*He looks at Sandra*) She?

CARBOY. Learn your place, my girl!

TEETER. Hush. She is ignorant. One must be tolerant.

CARBOY. Half Irish. It's no good.

TEETER (*to Sandra*) Come here, my child. (*He crosses and sits on the sofa*)

(SANDRA *rises and crosses to Teeter, head bowed, crying*)

Sit at my feet.

(SANDRA *sits on the floor at Teeter's feet*)

What is troubling you?

(SANDRA *cries quietly*)

CARBOY. Speak up, my girl!

TEETER. Tolerance, tolerance. Look at me, child.

(SANDRA *looks up at Teeter*)

Open your heart.

SANDRA. Is it . . . ? (*She hesitates*)

TEETER. What, child?

SANDRA. The end, sir?

CARBOY. Nonsense, nonsense!

TEETER. Hush. One moment. (*He rises, crosses to* L, *picks his way through what were the french windows, plucks a blade of grass, returns, sits on the sofa and hands the blade of grass to Sandra*)

SANDRA. A blade of grass?

TEETER (*pointing off* L) Look out there.

(SANDRA *looks off* L)

Do you see where I picked it?

SANDRA. No, sir.

TEETER. How many blades are left?

SANDRA. I don't know, sir.

TEETER. Count them.

SANDRA. I can't, sir.

TEETER. Why not?

SANDRA. There are too many, sir.

TEETER. Shall I put this blade back to fill up the space?

SANDRA. No, sir.

TEETER. Why not?

SANDRA. It doesn't notice, sir.

TEETER. Very good.

SANDRA. But what about the thrushes, sir?

TEETER. It works with thrushes, too.

SANDRA. Oh.

TEETER. Do you understand?

SANDRA. No, sir.

CARBOY. I tell you it's no good.

TEETER. Hush. Listen, my child. What is the relationship between this blade of grass in your hand, and that lawn?

SANDRA. Relationship?

TEETER. Suppose I make this blade of grass disappear. What will happen to the lawn?

SANDRA. Nothing, sir.

TEETER. Suppose I make the whole of the lawn disappear but one growing blade of grass. What will happen to that blade?

SANDRA. Sir?

TEETER. Will it grow more, or less, or the same as before?

CARBOY. More. It'll have more space. Unless the moles get it.

(TEETER *sighs*)

That is, if moles eat grass.

SANDRA. It's too complex, sir.

TEETER. All is for the best, my child. All is as it should be. To be otherwise is impossible. Do you understand?

SANDRA. Thrushes, squirrels . . .

TEETER (*rising*) Thrushes, squirrels, grass, trees. All must pass. We, too, we, too. What else would you have?

(SANDRA *is puzzled*)

CARBOY. You're wasting your time.

TEETER. Consider a growing flower . . .

(DAPHNE *enters* R, *carrying a tray with four cups of cocoa*)

DAPHNE (*crossing and putting the tray on the table* C) Cocoa for all.

CARBOY. Ah, you see?

DAPHNE. The last we'll get from *that* kitchen. (*She hands a cup of cocoa to Carboy*) And where Helen's to sleep tonight I can't imagine. (*She hands a cup of cocoa to Sandra*) However, it'll probably solve itself. (*She takes a cup of cocoa for herself*) Wandsworth, how nice to see you again. And I seem to have one cup over. (*She sits in the armchair* LC)

TEETER (*crossing and taking the last cup of cocoa*) There is a providence, you see . . .

DAPHNE. I think it may be a hot summer. If only the sun keeps going.

(*They sip their cocoa appreciatively, except for* SANDRA *who still sits dazed*)

CARBOY. Ah—it's the little things in life which make all the difference.

TEETER. No, no, it's the flow. It's the flow which matters. The *flow*. ·If we can keep going, if we can just keep going . . .

DAPHNE. For long enough.

CARBOY. Why not? We've got this far. (*He stretches out*

his arms, looks down at his feet and laughs) Look! No hands!

TEETER. Exactly. (*To Sandra*) Drink your cocoa, my child.

(SANDRA *sobs*)

DAPHNE. Drink it up, Sandra.
CARBOY. Drink it up, my girl!

(SANDRA *sips her cocoa*)

And be thankful.

CURTAIN

FURNITURE AND PROPERTY LIST

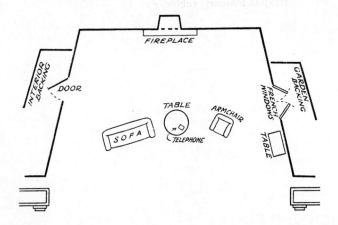

On stage : Table (c) *On it :* telephone, copy of the *Spectator*
           Sofa (RC) *On it :* cushions
           Armchair (LC)
           Table (down L)
           Window curtains
           Carpet on floor
           Over mantelpiece : large gilt-framed portrait of a Caroline
               drinking party
           Electric wall-brackets
           Other suitable dressing

Off stage : Dead mole (CARBOY)
           Bunch of flowers (DAPHNE)
           Secateurs (DAPHNE)
           Trolley. *On it :* an enormous vase (SANDRA)
           Blade of grass (TEETER)
           Tray. *On it :* 4 cups of cocoa (DAPHNE)

Personal: CARBOY: box of matches

During BLACK-OUT:
Strike: French windows and adjacent flats

Set: Heap of masonry, rubble, etc. (L)

LIGHTING PLOT

Property fittings required: Wall-brackets (not practical)
    Interior. A drawing-room. The same scene throughout

THE APPARENT SOURCE OF LIGHT is french windows L

THE MAIN ACTING AREAS are RC, C, LC and L

To open: Effect of morning sunshine

Cue 1   A picture falls   (Page 17)
          Black-Out

Cue 2   CARBOY: "As indeed he was."   (Page 18)
          Bring up lights as at opening

EFFECTS PLOT

Cue 1   At rise of CURTAIN   (Page 1)
Sound of two thrushes singing

Cue 2   HELEN looks up at sky   (Page 1)
Sound of a shot
One thrush stops singing abruptly

Cue 3   Follows above cue   (Page 1)
Sound of a shot
Second thrush stops singing abruptly

Cue 4   DAPHNE: ". . . or one large."   (Page 7)
Telephone rings

Cue 5   TEETER: ". . . unquestioning, blissful
                       sings."   (Page 10)
Sound of a shot

Cue 6   CARBOY: ". . . lawn and you . . ."   (Page 12)
A long, sad, rumbling sound culminating in a crash.
     A piece of plaster falls from the ceiling

Cue 7   CARBOY: ". . . fell in, you said . . ."   (Page 13)
A long sad, rumbling sound culminating in a crash.
     A piece of plaster falls from the ceiling

Cue 8   HELEN: ". . . no-one else knows."   (Page 16)
A crash

Cue 9   CARBOY: "Remember your place!"   (Page 17)
A crash. Plaster falls from the ceiling

Cue 10   HELEN: ". . . members of my family."   (Page 17)
A tremendous crash. A picture falls

Cue 11   CARBOY: ". . . sense of proportion."   (Page 18)
A crash of falling masonry

Cue 12   CARBOY: "... of the situation."   (Page 18)
            A crash of falling masonry

Cue 13   CARBOY: "... our mental limitations."   (Page 18)
            A crash of falling masonry and a scream cut short